Germ...y

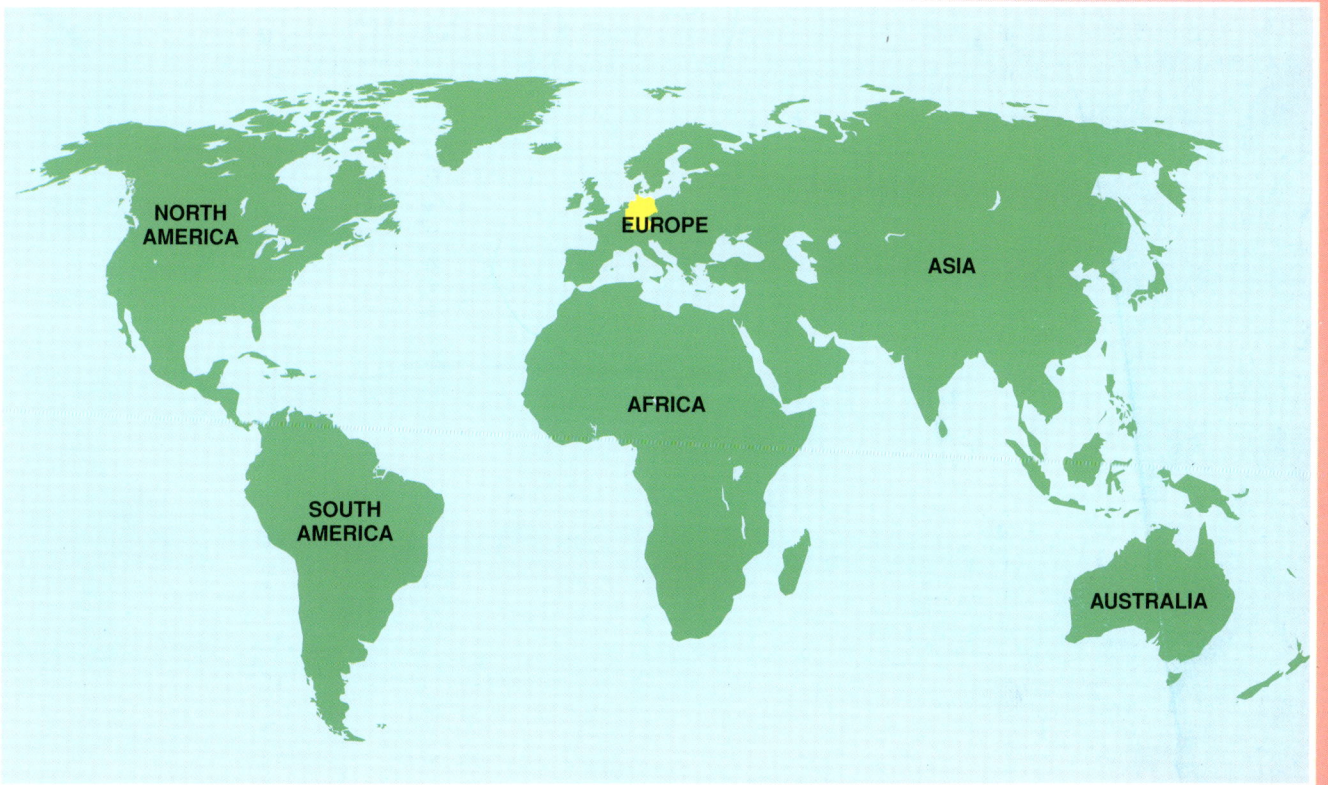

Fred Martin

Heinemann
LIBRARY

First published in Great Britain by Heinemann Library
Halley Court, Jordan Hill, Oxford OX2 8EJ
a division of Reed Educational and Professional Publishing Ltd

OXFORD FLORENCE PRAGUE MADRID ATHENS
MELBOURNE AUCKLAND KUALA LUMPUR SINGAPORE TOKYO
IBADAN NAIROBI KAMPALA JOHANNESBURG GABORONE
PORTSMOUTH NH CHICAGO MEXICO CITY SAO PAULO

Designed by AMR
Illustrations by Art Construction
Printed and bound in Italy by L.E.G.O.

02 01 00 99 98
10 9 8 7 6 5 4 3 2 1

ISBN 0 431 01347 0
This title is also available in a hardback library edition (ISBN 0 431 01346 2).

British Library Cataloguing in Publication Data

Martin, Fred, 1948-
Next Stop Germany
1. Germany – Geography – Juvenile literature
I.Title II.Germany
914.3

Acknowledgements
The Publishers would like to thank the following for permission to reproduce photographs:
J. Allan Cash pp.7, 8; Art Directors p.4; Trevor Clifford pp.10, 12–13, 16–17, 25; Colorific! Reinhard Janke/focus p.27, Alon Reininger/Contact p.18, Peter Turnley/Black Star p.28, Michael Yamashita p.24; Robert Harding Picture Library p.11; Katz Pictures Nascimento/Rea p.15, Tom Stoddart p.5; Spectrum Colour Library p.29; Trip David Cumming pp.14, 19, 22, Eric Smith p.26, R Styles p.6; A Tovy p.9, Trip p.23.

Cover photograph reproduced with permission of Zefa/Spichtinger.

Our thanks to Melissa Nuth for her comments in the preparation of this book.

Every effort has been made to contact holders of any material reproduced in this book. Any omissions will be rectified in subsequent printings if notice is given to the Publisher.

CONTENTS

GERMANY: PAST AND PRESENT

The fairy-tale castle at Neuschwanstein [noi-shvan-shtine] in Bavaria, south Germany.

- *The castle was built by King Ludwig II in the 19th century.*

A brief history

The River Rhine in Germany used to be the northern boundary of the **Roman Empire**. In AD400, the Roman army was forced to retreat. In AD410, Rome itself was attacked by Germanic Huns.

Germany then became part of Charlemagne's empire. This broke up in AD888 when the present area of Germany became a separate kingdom. For hundreds of years, many of the cities mostly ruled themselves. By 1701, a new kingdom of Prussia was formed. In 1871 Otto von Bismarck formed a new country that was to become most of modern Germany.

War and division

Germany fought and was defeated in World War I. Adolf Hitler became Germany's leader in 1933. In 1939, World War II began when Germany invaded Poland. By 1945, Germany had been defeated again.

In 1949 Germany was divided into two countries: East Germany and West Germany. The city of Berlin was also divided into two. East Germany, East Berlin and other countries in Eastern Europe were ruled by **communist** governments. A boundary line called the **iron curtain** divided the whole of Europe into east and west. In 1961, a concrete wall was built across Berlin to stop people moving between the two parts of the city.

City Population
- over 1,000,000
- over 500,000
- capital

0   200 km

When the East German government collapsed in 1989, people on both sides began to tear down the Berlin Wall themselves. Pieces of concrete from the Berlin Wall are now sold as souvenirs.

The fall of the Berlin Wall.
- *People celebrated as friends and relations were reunited.*
- *By 1990, there was only one German flag as East Germany and West Germany were joined to make one country again.*

United again

In 1990, the two parts of Germany were reunited to become the Federal Republic of Germany. People all over the world celebrated when the Berlin Wall was taken down in 1989.

Today most people in Germany have a good **standard of living**. Some in the east are not so lucky because factories and other businesses have closed down and there are a lot of people out of work. It may be some time before all the people in Germany can share in the same high standard of living.

THE NATURAL LANDSCAPE

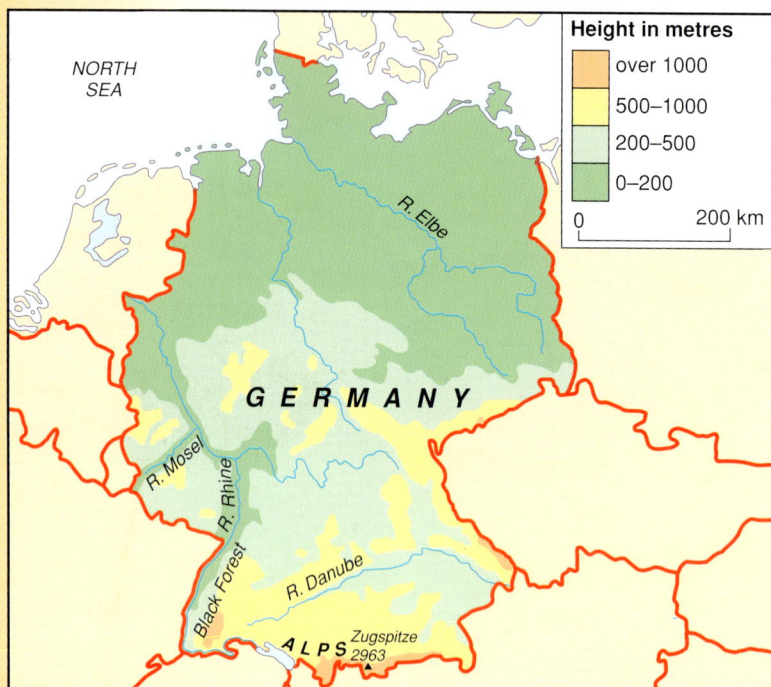

Height in metres

	over 1000
	500–1000
	200–500
	0–200

0   200 km

NORTH SEA

GERMANY

R. Elbe

R. Mosel

R. Rhine

Black Forest

R. Danube

ALPS   Zugspitze 2963

Rivers and valleys

Germany is the fifth largest country in Western Europe. It has a coastline along both the North Sea and the Baltic Sea. Some of Europe's longest rivers flow through Germany. The Bodensee (also called Lake Constance) covers 541 square kilometres and is 66 kilometres long.

The landscape across the north of Germany is part of the much larger North European Plain. This is a lowland area with wide river valleys, moors and low hills. The rivers Elbe, Rhine, Ems and Weser flow across these lowlands and make **estuaries** as they enter the North Sea.

Sometimes these rivers overflow, as in January 1995, when the Rhine flooded after a long period of heavy rain.

The steep-sided valley of the River Moselle.
- *The Moselle is a tributary of the River Rhine.*
- *It enters the Rhine from the west at Koblenz.*

The north of Germany is part of the much larger North European Plain.

- *The landscape is mostly low-lying land that is flat or has gentle slopes.*
- *Wide rivers with broad valleys meander across the landscape.*

The uplands

South of the lowlands, there are mountains and flat-topped uplands called **plateaux**. The highest peak is Brocken in the Hartz Mountains at 1142 metres. Some of the mountains are made from ancient and hard volcanic rocks.

Rivers have cut deeply into the mountains and plateaux. The Rhine has cut a deep and steep-sided valley called a **gorge**. The rivers Moselle, Main and Lahn are **tributaries** of the Rhine. They have also cut deep and winding gorges.

Spectacular Germany

The southern part of Germany is mainly hills and mountains. The River Danube has its **source** in the Black Forest uplands. The Rhine has its source in the Alps, flows through Switzerland, then into the Bodensee. From there, it flows north through Germany in a wide, deep valley. The uplands rise steeply near Austria to form the Bavarian Alps. The Zugspitze, at 2963 metres, is the highest peak in Germany. Steep slopes, snow and ice make this a spectacular landscape.

The River Rhine flows for 865 kilometres through Germany. The River Danube is longer at 2850 kilometres, but it only flows for 647 kilometres through Germany. The rest flows east to the Black Sea through Austria, Hungary and Romania.

7

CLIMATE, VEGETATION AND WILDLIFE

People enjoying the summer sunshine in Berlin.
- *Winters in Berlin are cold.*
- *Some weeks in the summer can be hot and dry with an average of 8 hours of sunshine per day in June and July.*

Weather and winds

People in Germany cope with all kinds of weather. In winter, when the temperature drops to below **freezing point**, they have to wrap up to keep warm and dry. In summer, there can be weeks of dry weather when the temperature is about 20°C. The areas with most summer sunshine are mainly in the south. The mountain areas are always colder and wetter than the lowlands.

Winds that blow over Germany come from all directions. In winter, very cold air with snow sometimes blows from Eastern Europe and from Asia. Icy air also blows down from the north.

Winds from the west blow in from the Atlantic Ocean. This air is usually warmer, and it is also likely to bring more rain. Winds from the south are blocked by the Alps. A special warm dry wind called the *Föhn* [fern] sometimes blows across southern Germany from the Alps. Cold dry air becomes warmer as it moves towards lower ground.

Woods and heath

Germany is one of Europe's most wooded countries. There are areas of **deciduous trees** such as oak and birch in the lowlands. In the uplands, there are vast areas of fir trees. These dark trees give the Black Forest in southern Germany its name.

Most land in the lowlands has been cleared of its natural vegetation so that it can be farmed or used to build towns and cities. However, the area called the Luneburg Heath is largely untouched. The soil is thin and stoney, so it is no good for farming. Heather and other wild shrubs grow here.

Protecting the environment

Large species of wildlife, such as deer and wild boar, live mainly in the upland forests. These forests are being conserved in ten **National Parks**. A major problem is that **acid rain** is killing the trees in more than half the country's forests. The only answer to this is to reduce the amount of air **pollution** throughout Europe.

About 30% of land in Germany is covered in forest. In the Rhineland-Palatinate state in the south-west, just over 40% of the land is forest. This is about 8000 square kilometres, almost the same size as the whole of Cyprus.

The Black Forest landscape in the south of Germany.
- *The land is higher in the south than in the north.*
- *Dark green coniferous trees grow in the Black Forest.*

TOWNS AND CITIES

The historic town of Passau in the south of Germany.

- *There has been a town on this site for over 2000 years, since Celtic times.*
- *The Romans built a settlement in the same place.*
- *It is now a port for barges that sail up the River Danube.*

Berlin the capital

Before World War II, Berlin was Germany's **capital city**. Like most big German cities, large areas of it were destroyed by bombing and fighting during the war. After the war it was divided up by the allied armies into East and West Berlin, with the USSR controlling East Berlin. The Berlin Wall was built in 1961. East Berlin became the capital of East Germany and Bonn became the capital of West Germany.

Since 1945, old buildings in Berlin have been restored and new ones have been built. In 1990, it became joint capital with Bonn of the newly united Germany. It will become the only capital in the year 2000.

Industrial towns and ports

Germany was one of the countries in Europe where there was an **industrial revolution** during the last century. Towns and cities grew where coal and iron ore were mined. The changes had most impact in an area now called the Ruhr. A band of industrial towns stretches about 100 kilometres from east to west. Some towns, such as Essen and Duisburg [dois-bourg], have grown so big that there is almost no land left between them. A built-up area like this is called a **conurbation**.

Barges carrying **freight** sail on rivers such as the Rhine and Elbe. This has made towns such as Duisburg, Cologne and Koblenz into inland ports with docks, factories and other businesses. Sea ports such as Hamburg and Bremen have grown where the rivers reach the sea.

The Brandenburg Gate in the centre of Berlin is one of the city's most famous landmarks. It was completed in 1791. It was built to look like a building from ancient Greece.

Country towns

There are hundreds of small, attractive country towns all over Germany. They are popular places with tourists and city dwellers who come to visit for local festivals. Small towns near to big cities have also become places where **commuters** like to live.

The town square and Christmas market at Nuremberg in southern Germany.
- *Nuremberg is one of Germany's historic towns.*
- *Much of it had to be rebuilt after the Second World War.*
- *There is an international toy fair at Nuremberg every year.*

SUBURBAN LIFE IN GERMANY

The Berger family

The five members of the Berger family live in Esslingen on the edge of the city of Stuttgart. Esslingen is a mainly **residential** area that has been built up in recent years. The family live in one of ten flats in a block. Theirs is on the top floor. Many German families live in flats and not in individual houses. Markus and Heike [hiker] Berger moved to live there two years after the birth of their first children, Ruth and Hannah. The two girls are identical twins, aged six. The youngest member of the family is their brother Jonathan, who is only one year old.

The family's day

Markus Berger is aged 35. He works as a manager in a factory that makes parts for machinery. They sell some of their products to the Lego company in Denmark, to help make Lego building blocks. The factory is not too far away, so Markus keeps himself fit by cycling to work every day. It only takes him ten minutes to get there.

The Berger family outside their home.

Baby Jonathan is not left out when the family go for cycle rides.

A shopping centre in Esslingen.
• This is a modern part of Stuttgart where local people do their weekly shopping.

The family's evening meal.
- *Spaghetti bolognese with Parmesan cheese is on the menu this evening.*

Markus Berger cycles to work every day.

Heike Berger is two years younger than Markus. She does not go out to work but she may find another job when the children are a little older. For the moment, she has more than enough to do looking after the children, especially baby Jonathan. She also does the housework and goes shopping in the local shopping centre and supermarket.

The twins go to a kindergarten school every day. They are there from 9.00 am until 12.00 noon, then they go home for lunch. After lunch, they go back to the school again until 4.00 pm. Their favourite foods are pasta and chocolate puddings.

Out and about

The family sometimes go cycling together. Baby Jonathan is strapped into a special trailer at the back of Heike's bike. Markus also enjoys rock climbing. He sometimes does this in an old quarry near Stuttgart.

The countryside around Stuttgart is pleasant. It attracts tourists who come for walks and other types of recreation. Living in this part of Germany can help give people a better quality of life than in some of the older industrial areas further north.

Heike does most of her shopping in the local supermarket.
- *She drives the goods home in the family car.*

FARMING LANDSCAPES

Farm work

Only about 5 out of every 100 people work on farms in Germany. This is normal for a rich country such as Germany. In poor countries, as many as 80 out of every 100 people may work in farming. But even in Germany, farming is still important, not only because people have to be fed, but also because it is an important part of the country's environment and landscape.

Farm produce

Germany is in the world's top ten producers of wheat, barley, oats, potatoes, sugar beet, hops and rape seed oil. Growing crops such as these is called **arable** farming. Growing **grain crops**, such as wheat and barley, is a special type of arable farming.

More hops and barley are grown in Germany than in any other country. Hops and barley are used to make beer. Only the USA makes more beer than Germany. There are also vineyards in Germany, where grapes are grown to make wine. Grapes are usually grown on steep south-facing slopes to catch more sun. Germany is the seventh largest producer of wine in the world. Germany is also one of the world's biggest livestock farmers of pigs, cattle and chickens.

Grapes are grown in vineyards on the steep slopes of the Rhine gorge.
- *The sun's heat is greatest on south-facing slopes.*
- *This area is best known for white wines.*

The warm summer climate is also good for growing fruits such as plums, apples and pears. These are grown in orchards. Forestry covers a lot of land in Germany. Trees are grown for their wood, and replaced when they are cut down. This ensures more wood for the future.

Farm business

In East Germany after 1949, all farms were run by the government as **co-operatives**. Now people can own their own farms again. Some farmers have joined up to run their own co-operatives.

In western Germany, many farms are too small to be profitable and need more machinery to make them efficient. About 70% of all the farms are under 50 hectares in size. This is less than half the size of an average UK farm.

Making farming more modern will not be easy. Many people will lose their jobs because there will be fewer, but bigger, farms and more machinery to do the work that used to be done by people.

About 40% of the farmers in Germany are part-time farmers. This means that they have to do another job as well as farming to earn a decent living.

RURAL GERMANY

The forest ranger

Hans Gaisbauer works as a forest ranger in one of the largest forest areas in Germany. This is the Bavarian Forest in the south of Germany, near the border with Austria. Timber is an important industry in this part of Germany. The Gaisbauer family live in a detached house on the edge of the town of Passau.

Hans usually works from 7.00 am until about 4.00 pm. He is in charge of a team of seven other workers. Their job is to fell the older trees, protect the young ones and plant new ones for the future. There are both **deciduous** and **coniferous trees** in the forest. These include species such as beech, maple, ash, pine, birch and larch. The forest is also rich in birds and other wildlife that need to be protected and **conserved**.

Hans Gaisbauer at work in the forest.
- *It is autumn time. It is becoming colder and the leaves are starting to fall.*

Ute is learning to play the recorder.

Gisela shopping in the market.
- *Apples and vegetables are grown in the local area, but other foods come from other parts of Germany and from abroad.*

The evening meal of Schnitzel with mashed potatoes and salad.
• The carved pumpkin in the window shows it is Hallowe'en.

The three children have a big garden with a cage for their pet rabbits.
• They thought they had two female rabbits, but they were wrong!

Gisela at work and home

Gisela Gaisbauer works as a part-time English teacher in a local secondary school. As well as her work at school, she also does the family cooking. One of the family's favourite meals is a local dish called *Scheinsgraten*. This is a meat loaf with a sauce that is usually eaten with potato dumplings. She travels to the market in Passau once a week to buy fresh food.

The Gaisbauer children

Hans and Gisela have three children. Ute, the eldest girl, is thirteen. Felix is eleven and Almut is their youngest daughter, aged eight. Ute walks to school. The two other children go to school by bus like many other children who live in the countryside. The journey takes about 20 minutes. Their school day lasts from 8.00 am until 1.00 pm. When they get home, there is always homework to be done.

For recreation, the family sometimes goes walking in the forest. They also enjoy playing cards and board games. Ute is learning to play the recorder and both she and Felix are learning to play the piano. Making and playing musical instruments is one of the traditions in this part of Germany.

The three children are going off to school.
• Two of them go by bus to their schools in Passau.

WHAT'S IN GERMAN SHOPS?

A covered shopping mall in Hamburg.
- *It is just like any other shopping mall anywhere else in the world!*

Big store shopping

Shopping in Germany is similar in many ways to how people do their shopping in the United Kingdom. There are supermarkets in towns and much bigger **hypermarkets** in all the main German cities.

A new trend has been for shopping in warehouses where shelves are stacked high and prices are kept low.

There is space for up to 5000 cars in the car parks of the biggest hypermarkets. It is usually easier to park a car at a supermarket than in a city centre. Also, car parks at supermarkets are free, unlike car parks in the city centre.

City centre shopping

There are department stores and a variety of smaller specialist shops such as jewellers and clothes shops in the city centres. Many of the city centres had to be rebuilt after World War II. Some streets were made into **pedestrian precincts** where cars are not allowed. These are attractive places for shoppers because they provide more space, pleasant sitting areas and open-air cafés. Shopping is more pleasant without the danger of having to cross the road and breathe in traffic fumes.

A shopping street in Cologne.
- *This street has been made into a pedestrian precinct where vehicles are not allowed.*
- *Shoppers can sit at tables outside cafés.*

German shops are known for being environmentally friendly because they rarely use disposable plastic carrier bags. *Der Grüne Punkt* [gruner pungkt] is a symbol that indicates packaging which can be recycled. Customers in supermarkets can even take their goods out of the packaging before taking them home!

There are open-air markets in the main squares and nearby streets of many historic towns and cities in Germany. The weeks before Christmas are a special time for shopping in these markets.

Specialist shops

Many small local shops have closed down in places where supermarkets have been opened. Some, however, have managed to stay open. They have done this by selling more specialist goods or better quality, more expensive goods. This sort of shop sells many types of goods such as meat, toys, cakes and clothes. Smaller shops also offer a more personal service which many customers like.

Many German people still prefer to buy their fresh food from local shops. For instance, they prefer to buy bread from their local bakers. They like to eat it fresh from a baker's oven rather than made in a factory then sliced and wrapped in plastic.

19

GERMAN COOKING

Traditional food

In Germany, each region has its own traditional food. This is because the food eaten in each region is made from local produce, perhaps from the local farm or from the Baltic and North Sea fishing grounds. Some German foods have become internationally famous, such as frankfurters, which are a type of sausage which originated in Frankfurt, or Black Forest gâteau.

Main meals

Fish dishes are made mainly in the north near the fishing ports where herring, eels, prawns and a range of white fish are caught. *Hamburger Aalsuppe* [arlzupper], a fish soup from Hamburg, and rollmops are popular in northern cities. Rollmops are strips of salted herring mixed with spices, onions and gherkins.

Germans eat many types of meat including ham, pork and beef. *Leberkäse* [layber-kayzer] is a meat loaf made of beef and pork that is popular in southern Germany. There are many kinds of sausage, including *Weißwurst* [vice-vourst], a sausage that is white. In Germany, each person eats more meat on average than people in most other countries.

Radishes and other fresh vegetables on sale in a street market.
- *Locally grown produce is used to make traditional recipes.*

There are many types of bread available in Germany.
- *German people prefer to eat freshly baked bread made from the flour of their choice.*

Other favourites are *Sauerkraut* [zower-krowt] (pickled cabbage) and *Sauerbraten* (pot-roast meat) which were first made hundreds of years ago as a way of preserving the foods. Potatoes, dumplings and green vegetables are part of most main meals.

In Germany there are many different types of bread. One called *Pumpernickel* is made with rye flour or a mixture of rye and wheat.

Fruit, cakes and drink

Cakes made from apples and other fruits are often eaten in the afternoon with coffee. Apple *Strudel* and Black Forest gâteau are two favourites. Doughnuts are a speciality in Berlin.

Grapes are grown to make different types of white wine such as *Hock* and *Liebfraumilch*. There are also stronger drinks such as *Schnapps*, a type of gin.

There are at least 5000 different types of beer brewed in Germany. On average, each person in southern Germany drinks 250 litres of beer each year. This is twice as much as the average person in the United Kingdom.

MADE IN GERMANY

World leaders

Germany is one of the world's top ten producers of **manufactured** goods. These goods include cars, ships, steel, electrical equipment, machinery and chemicals. Manufacturing is the main way in which Germany has become one of the world's richest countries.

Inventions by Karl Benz and Gottlieb Daimler in 1885 and by Rudolf Diesel in 1892 helped Germany become a leading country for making motor cars.

Coal, metal and energy

Coal from the Ruhr was used to start off Germany's **industrial revolution**. This helped build up an iron and steel industry. At first, local iron ore was used. Now it has to be brought to Germany from other countries. The iron and steel is used to make all sorts of metal goods such as machinery, trains and ships.

Mining brown coal called lignite near Aachen in the west of Germany.
- *Lignite is mined from near the surface by open-cast methods.*
- *The coal is burnt in power stations to generate electricity.*

The BMW car assembly factory in Regensburg in Bavaria.

- *Robots and other machines are used to build high-quality cars on the production line.*

Most of the coal that is mined is lignite. Lignite is a poor form of coal, but it burns well in power stations to give electricity. Some power stations in Germany are powered by nuclear energy.

Industry today

Germany is the third largest car producer in the world. It is fifth for making chemicals from oil. Skilled German workers also make electronic goods such as televisions and scientific instruments that are highly accurate. Names such as Siemens, Bosch and AEG are known all over the world for high-quality engineering in electrical goods. Germans understand that **technology** is an important way to keep the country rich.

There are factories in all of the big German cities. They produce things ranging from ships in Hamburg, to aircraft in Munich. Many of the new industries have set up in cities in the south, such as Augsburg and Regensburg. It is more pleasant to live and work in these cities which are near the countryside, rather than in the older industrial cities of the Ruhr.

The company that employs more workers than any other in Germany is Daimler-Benz. The workforce of over 376,000 people makes cars and different types of electrical goods.

TRANSPORT AND TRAVEL

By road and rail

The first *Autobahn*, or motorway, was built in Germany about 50 years ago. There are no speed limits on most stretches of the motorways, though motorists are advised not to travel at over 130 kilometres per hour. All of the main cities are linked by motorways. This makes it easy to travel from place to place. A car journey of about 500 kilometres from Berlin to Munich should take about five or six hours.

All the big cities are linked by high-speed railways. There is usually one train every hour between them. The high-speed InterCity Express trains (ICE) travel at 280 kilometres per hour. Trains are also used by **commuters** who travel from the outskirts of the cities and from the countryside into the city centres to work.

There are good bus and tram services in all the major cities. There are underground services in the biggest cities such as in Berlin and Munich.

An **Autobahn** *near Berlin.*

- *In Germany, more goods and people travel by road than by any other means of transport.*

Old trams still run along the streets of Stuttgart.
• *The power comes from overhead electricity cables.*

Boats and planes

All of the biggest rivers in Germany are **navigable**. Including the canals, this makes a total of 6900 kilometres of navigable waterways. There are just under 4000 barges in use in Germany. Barges are used because they are the cheapest way of carrying bulky cargoes, such as coal or iron ore. A canal has been built to link the Rhine to the Danube so that barges can sail all the way from the North Sea to the Black Sea.

There are flights between the biggest cities for people who need to travel faster. The flying time between Berlin and Munich is only 1 hour and 20 minutes. Flying always costs more than travel by road or rail but it is quick. This is important to people in business.

The strangest looking railway is in Wuppertal near Cologne. Carriages hang down from overhead metal pylons. This railway was built almost 100 years ago and is still running!

LEISURE, SPORT AND HOLIDAYS

Money to spend

People in Germany take their play as seriously as their work. Most of them earn enough money and have enough spare time to enjoy themselves.

At home, people do much the same as people in most other wealthy countries. They watch television, play computer games or read books and magazines.

For a night out, there are cafés, discos and theatres. Berlin is famous for its night-clubs and restaurants. A *Bierkeller* is a bar where people meet to drink and sing. This is a special tradition in the south of Germany.

Theme parks and sport

For a day out, there are large recreation parks with play equipment, swimming pools and adventure trails. Some of these have been built on old industrial land. *Phantasialand* near Cologne is a **theme park** where there are roller-coaster rides and theatres with music and magic shows. You can walk down streets that look like the American Wild West or Berlin in the 1930s.

Hang-gliding in the mountains of Bavaria.

- *Bavaria is one of the most popular tourist areas of Germany.*
- *It is a clean mountain environment with many sporting opportunities, including skiing.*

Tennis, football, gymnastics and skiing are popular sports both to play and to watch. Water sports are enjoyed on the rivers and lakes. More than 21 million people are members of sports clubs in Germany. This is one person in every four.

Coast and country

The coastlines of the Baltic Sea and the North Sea become crowded with holidaymakers in summer, though many Germans prefer to go abroad for a seaside holiday. Tourists also like to visit the Black Forest and the Bavarian Alps. The woodland landscape in the Black Forest makes it ideal for walking and camping holidays. Skiing is a popular type of winter holiday in the Alps. The Rhine gorge and Moselle valley are popular areas to visit because of their small towns, vineyards and attractive river landscapes.

There are many castles and medieval towns in Germany. The Neuschwanstein Castle in Bavaria, south Germany, is one of the best-known castles. Trier, on the River Moselle, is said to be the oldest town in Germany. It used to be the ancient Roman capital of Germany.

The world-class German national football team has been very successful in international competitions. Delighted fans have watched Germany win the World Cup three times.

Football fans at a cup final in Berlin.
- *The German Football Federation is the biggest sports organization in Germany.*

CUSTOMS AND ARTS

Enjoying some glasses of beer at the Munich Oktoberfest.
* *The men are wearing traditional hats and leather trousers, called* Lederhosen.

Tales and legends

Everyone enjoys a good story and some of the best stories come from Germany. *The Pied Piper of Hamelin* is the story of a town in Germany which was cleared of rats by a pipe player who also took all the children away. *Hansel and Gretel*, *Rapunzel* and other stories were collected and written down by two brothers, Jakob and Wilhelm Grimm, almost 200 years ago.

Festival time

The Christmas tradition of Santa Claus bringing presents began in Germany. It came from stories about Saint Nikolaus. The idea of having Christmas trees decorated with lights also comes from Germany.

There are other religious festivals in Germany, such as the Oberammergau Passion Play which began in 1634. It is only performed once every ten years. The play tells the story of the life of Jesus. About 500 townspeople take part in the play and it lasts for almost seven hours.

The Munich *Oktoberfest* is a very different kind of festival. This celebrates harvest time, but it has also become known as a beer festival.

Music and art

Many famous composers and artists were born in Germany. Beethoven, Wagner and Bach are three of the most famous composers of classical music. There are world-famous orchestras in Berlin, Leipzig, Dresden and Munich. About half of all school children in Germany play a musical instrument and there are at least 15,000 choirs to be found throughout the country.

Holbein and Dürer are famous artists of both paintings and woodcuts. They both lived in the late 1400s and early 1500s. In the present century, *Bauhaus*, a famous German architecture movement which ran from 1919 to 1939, influenced the appearance of much of what we see around us today, from our streets and city buildings to our daily newspapers.

The children's festival in Dinkelsbühl.
- *Music, dancing, parades and games celebrate the liberation from the Swedes in 1632.*
- *Legend tells how a group of children met the enemy outside the city walls to beg for peace – and so the Swedes agreed and left them alone.*

Saint Nikolaus was a bishop who was famous for his kindness to children. One night he left three pieces of gold on the mantelpiece for three poor girls. The gold rolled into the girls' stockings that had been hung up to dry and so began the tradition for hanging up Christmas stockings.

GERMANY FACTFILE

Area 356,950 square kilometres

Highest point Zugspitze 2963 m

Climate

	January temp.	July temp.	Total annual rainfall
Berlin	0°C	17°C	720 mm

Population 82 million

Population density 235 people per square kilometre

Life expectancy
Female 78
Male 72

Capital city Berlin and Bonn

Population of the main cities (in millions)

Berlin	3.4
Hamburg	1.7
Munich	1.2
Cologne	1.0
Dortmund	0.6
Düsseldorf	0.6
Essen	0.6
Frankfurt	0.6
Stuttgart	0.6
Bremen	0.5

Land use

Farming	33%
Forest	30%
Grass	15%
Other	22%

Employment

Services	58%
Industry	39%
Farming	3%

Main imports
Machinery and transport equipment
Food and live animals
Chemicals
Petroleum products

Main exports
Machinery and transport equipment
Chemicals
Manufactured goods

Language

German	98%
Turkish	1%
Other	1%

Religions

Protestant	45%
Roman Catholic	37%
Muslim	2%
Other	16%

Money
1 Deutschmark = 100 pfennig

Wealth $23,560
(The total value of what is produced by the country in one year, divided by its population and converted into US dollars).

GLOSSARY

acid rain rainwater carrying air pollution chemicals that can rot rocks and kill vegetation

arable a type of farming that involves ploughing the land to grow crops

Autobahn motorway in Germany

capital city the city where a country has its government

communist communists believe that all property, especially land and businesses, should be owned by the state on behalf of all the country's people

commuter a person who regularly travels a long way to work

coniferous trees trees that have cones, such as pines, firs and yew

conserve to protect and keep for future people to see and enjoy

conurbation a very large built-up area formed when two or more cities meet

co-operatives farms that are owned by several people who work together and take a share in the profits

deciduous trees trees that shed their leaves at the end of their growing season

estuary the wide tidal mouth of a river

freezing point 0°C, the point at which water becomes frozen

freight goods transported in containers

gorge a deep and narrow valley cut by a river

grain crops crops such as wheat and barley which produce grain

hypermarket the largest type of supermarket

industrial revolution a period at the end of the 18th century when machines were invented which could do a lot of the work previously done by people

iron curtain the former border between communist Eastern Europe and capitalist Western Europe

manufactured goods made in factories

National Park a large area of natural landscape that is conserved for wildlife and that tourists can visit

navigable a river that can be used by boats for transporting goods

pedestrian precinct a shopping street where cars are not allowed

plateaux flat-topped upland areas surrounded by steep slopes

pollution different ways in which air and water are made dirty

residential an area of a town or city where people live

Roman Empire the area once ruled by the Romans

source the place where a river starts to flow, usually a spring, lake or glacier

standard of living the measure of how well people live and eat in a country

technology the use of machinery and scientific skills

theme park a recreation area with adventure rides and activities

tributaries small rivers that join larger rivers

INDEX